rice

OTHER BOOKS BY JOAN LOGGHE

What Makes a Woman Beautiful
(Pennywhistle Press)

Twenty Years in Bed With the Same Man
(La Alameda Press)

Blessed Resistance
(Mariposa Printing & Publishing)

Sofia
(La Alameda Press)

Another Desert: Jewish Poetry of New Mexico
edited by Joan Logghe & Miriam Sagan
(Sherman Asher Press)

Joan Logghe

RICE

Tres Chicas Books

Thanks to these publications in which some of these poems previously appeared: "What about your children's skin," "Dead rattlesnake," "My friend says" in *The Rag;* "You gave me a love bite," in *Santa Fe Poetry Broadside;* "Is the world new," "Seems I might live," "My son who is twenty," *"Snowapple",* "In what was Safeway," *The Mending Wall;* "Gersh said," *Fish Drum;* " Didn't Buddha say," "Mother Theresa died," "An old postcard," "Thanksgiving Day," "She came back from Nepal, " *Lunarosity;* "You gave me a love bite," *In Company: An Anthology of New Mexico Poets after 1960,* University of New Mexico Press; "You gave me roses," *Chokecherries* 2003-2004.

Copyright © 2004 by Joan Logghe

Book design: JB Bryan & Renée Gregorio

Set in Weiss with Albertus titling

Cover art: "Bowl of Mountains" by Anonymous

Author photograph by Diane Ronayne

ISBN 1-893003-05-1

All Rights Reserved

Tres Chicas Books
12 C Eckards Way
Española, New Mexico 87532

The night I married all my friends sang for me,
And the rice of pleasure and the rice of pain fell on me.

— Kabir —

translated by Robert Bly

One night I wrote four poems on a long sheet of rice paper. I noticed they had a uniform shape and decided to give myself the pleasure of writing domestic sonnets. For two and a half years they spilled off of rice paper and into my computer. I have always played with how you can make art in the cracks of the daily, in this case the amount of time it takes for rice to cook, and at the end of the boiling, there is a poem. This book was held together by rice. It is as formal and formless as those grains, both cooked and uncooked. My grandson, recently eating take-out Chinese food, asked for "Mas clouds." His mix of Spanish and metaphor at age 20 months let me know that the allure of rice was endless, non-literal, and nourishing. I dedicate these poems to my brother and his wife, Carl and Carol Slesinger, who have been staples in my life.

My friend says, *You have everything!*
A house, three children, a man with a job.
All of this is true so how come some nights
can be filled with thanking and some fight-
ing. About what? Money? Alcohol? The soul?
It's not complaint when the apple, blameless,
with no trace of coddling moth is ruined
by the hail. It's fact, as our corn in tassel

eaten by cattle is outcome of open range.
The perfect longs to actuate, but flaw,
acts of God, bad weather, astrology,
some stray dog of a word, brings downfall,
nemesis to you. You bite the blemished apple,
drink well water tinted with rust, live another day.

It is painful to love as it is to give birth,
toil their heads out of the shaking.
Tourniquets for the infinite, this life
and death. Oblivion is a word I forbid!
My children come and go like moods.
What about your children's skin? she asks.
How can you live around such beauty?

My own father has no skin but mine.
I am sated with abundance, my family
around me all the time, a loving
and a holding. I am lucky. Blessed.
I fought the love off for a dozen years,
for two, finally relax into my calling.

My late father is visiting The White Place
so he can criticize the food. No melons
here, no Chinese, nothing like a rotisserie.
He hated when women from India pierced
their nose. We fought, one of the two fights
I recall. "It's cultural," I screamed,
in the revolving door of Carnegie Deli,
like neckties, hot pastrami, like taste in art.

Just about sunset I saw Georgia O'Keeffe
dog's shadow dart behind a rock. A chow.
Someone sold that shadow for seventy thou,
as if landscape can be bought. *Plaza Blanca*,
a very expensive fleeting moment, like this,
walking with three women towards my father.

On the eve of my birthday, my own
mother calls. She is walking on three legs
at sunset. It's Sabbath in her mouth.
She is blessing and blessing me
on the phone. I take these wishes
into my body. I try and absorb,
to become porous, an unglazed porcelain,
translucent, transparent, mild.

All that resistance of youth, gone.
Later on, I am counting the rain, digits.
I am letting my body go fifty.
Fifty. Thanking in the night, my mother alive,
playing golf the morning her sister dies.
The harder the contest, the better her game.

You gave me a love bite the week
I turned fifty, and I became like
all other women. The woman at Mustang
Gas. The woman who works
at Walgreens whose mother works at
Walgreens also. The women named for stars
and those named for hope. Women who love God
and worship inside and outside churches.

Those women who stand outside the house
and weep, and those whose body has failed
them and those who have failed their bodies.
All of these, bitten by love, as I
have been, unbeknownst to me on the week
I turned fifty.

I hold one human form which is as much
blessing as body, as much prayer
as genital. One man I love is seventy.
The nerve to die, four or five of you.
I passed a sad man on the road
who would have loved me. Ambition
flew out our window over there,
a haze over the Jemez. Leftover flies

from summer on the glass. I swoon
my way through autumn. Not the same
knocking or the same wood. Held and holy,
the heart is the tisket, the tasket, blood
basket. Full lotus position and then the casket.
Under the next full moon, let's just kiss.

The brilliant scholar can be tight with
money. The kind-hearted woman has no mind.
The lazy are perfect with children,
the beggar should never apologize.
A man tried to sell me a stolen hat.
Then God blessed me left and right
when I gave him a buck. The wad of money
stuffed into his pocket padded my guilt.

My parents taught charity all my life.
I forgot how to beg until now. In Tibetan
she said I'd make a good holy beggar.
My children ask for little, they are trained.
Our dogs know how to beg and die too soon.
Our cats live long. This life more purr than bark.

My innocence returned in the night.
Yesterday I rode a horse east as if a child.
The children are home for Thanksgiving, all three.
Suddenly, my glory is revealed to me. Family
all around, walking in and out the front door.
Eating their particular foods, loving people
I have no say about. Beautiful back
of my son, long hair of my progeny.

How easy it is to love children. But men
are a trickier love component. They come
into my body but did not come out of it. Men
have large heavy feet and lift them and put
them down on the stairs leading up.
I dwell in this simple complexity.

Like someone slightly biblical, I wake in full moon.
November is a time for crossing over, laughter
into early dark, breath into crying, health
into cough. My child has a weight on her chest,
one of many that she will dance under.
Allow this girl a golden life, perfect life.
I want to swallow her illness, spit out crystals,
reach into her chest and pull out substances.

For as long as she walks on the earth, her
face will shine me. I want an eternity
of how I love children, my issue, and
easy targets, love's arrow and its aim.
Love's accidents, the unfortunate repository
for flaws. Perfect myself for their small sakes.

When I learned Hebrew, serious and wise,
I pondered heaven, deconstructed war.
I walked the city, the avenues of sighs
and the pavements of commerce. I gave coins
to the afflicted on the corners. I read signs
about the end of the world. I had a calling
for serious living as other girls loved cats.
I let the prayers of my people confuse me.

I read about Anne Frank and horses. I read
that if parents eat sour grapes, their
children's teeth will be set on edge.
I popped a grape into my mouth by accident
when I was fasting. I was a child secretly
carrying World War II in my lunch box.

I gave up fasting for Lent, that was my
sacrifice. They said, heretic. I said,
"There a tick, there a tock, it's time
that is master." I refuse. I accept.
Invitations are cheap, it's time that
is dear. Today is the celebration
of cancellation. Cancel everything
not running towards you shouting, Great!

All day you make fate. Chickens cannot be
scolded into eggs. The wind never read
the ten commandments, covets everybody's
wife. The horse cannot be cajoled
into sleep. Women too sleep standing up.
This is written on rice.

In the course of a weekend the guppies die,
a transparent frog arrives by post. You cry
and draw a diagram of how it was last night
when I misspoke, tell me I lack balls. This you say
in Spanish so it has less yolk. I go on joking
and doing wash, cooking a meal or not. We play
married couple with healthy kids. We come true,
don't get the corn or beans in. I blame you

for all I fail in. A blue trial of love.
The world is blooming, yucca is the sword,
swash-buckling, used for everything from soap
to shampoo, to baskets of rope.
We view it for beauty. That's how I use
you in these north, south, east, west blues.

My son who is twenty today cut his hair
which had grown for years, long as
counterculture. He buzzed it. He says
he is a redneck, not a Jew. Why label?
My daughter, laughing, cuts through his
hair on the back porch. When he was one,
we moved here. I would wrap him as gift.
I would swaddle. This week he leaves again,

driving in an old car to the west. He'll learn
to fight fires, label stands of pines, walk
through clear cut and find a fawn. His hair
is now separate from his body, a little death
in it. He wants to sell it, someone else to wear him,
someone like you, who lost everything before leaving.

We will never see a season like this.
A wedding every week, a moon
dishing out gossip. Tell me about lovers
and angels who come to repair your sink.
Tell me about unfaithful and faithful men,
and why you think women are kinder
when actually we all swim upstream.
Time can be cruel, depending on the light.

This is the month heaven shifts onto the faces
of sunflowers, plates of seeds, color that curls
up and dies. Love till you drop, the moon confides.
I cry in public for the sake of pain. Suffering
is a fine way to lengthen an hour. Rejoice.
It's not as if you knew your life needed changing.

Labor Day, woke up from dreaming
of telling my dream to my friend who married
yesterday. She danced a legend at her wedding.
Her husband became all of our best loves.
I dreamed the Safeway checkout girl complained
that she worked more and more for good pay,
but she was an artist. Never did her thing.
I forgot that the dream's about me.

My husband called early from the firehouse,
up half the night fighting two fires, arson
in the mountain town of Cordova. I'd hoped
for a different fire, courted a different
tune. Then the blues lifted, Billie Holiday,
Ms. Brown, and all of us are smoke.

I dreamed of the work I have to do.
I dreamed my brother was carving wood,
my sister-in-law carving boxes. The rabbi
has us dancing at Yom Kippur. He said,
"Weeping is meditation, laughter is prayer."
The woman whose son was killed removed
the word "accident" from her dictionary.
God seats me in airplanes next to my teacher.

Who inhabits the next seat: my mother,
the nun, the saint, the Muslim girl,
the charlatan, the audience, a fool,
the maker of bombs? Out of the house I follow
Rilke, become vast, pray *zikhr*, no tomorrow.
Juanita says: these are the benefits of dreaming.

Ten of the nicest men walked into the bar.
I had been looking out the dream window,
plate glass at a view, new to eyeshot. Who
put those cliffs at right angles to earth?
Why these Ponderosa pine? Since when
was blue an invention of the mountains?
What refurbishes a confused heart?
I was palm reading God's hand.

He wanted to move gravel into holes
on the road where the rain's exuberance
had cut furrows, gullies, the rush of God.
He was longing to ride his horse all day
and asked me along. We walked an hour out,
an hour back, though he adores galloping.

Didn't Buddha say, "All is suffering?"
And Issa say, "The saddle is the same
as the zafu," and "The housewife and the monk
have a common job?" I left the water on.
I fold the socks mindlessly. Oh careless love.
Did Hari Das say, "The way of the householder
is not for everyone. Be householder saints!"
The demanding asks for just a little more.

The life I sought at twenty-five I attain
at double that. Midlife mystic. I chose this land,
the mornings are the same, the school lunch.
The same iris for a lifetime. I give up.
My children chose me and live with teeth
set on edge by my sour grapes. *Capiche?*

Mother Theresa died and you turned fifty-
two. Princess Diana's coffin travels to her gate.
Everything has the smell of making love,
I was going to say, amour. The dozen eggs
I pick, reaching under the broody hen,
the apple crisp I bake in honor of your birth.
The tree you planted that grew that sexy smell.
Amour, I was tempted to say that word again.

I cut the hail spots off the fruit, it's tart
and white fleshed. We have to prune, to cut,
to live with mighty imperfection. Can I say,
in America, the ruined words "I love you?" Now
that you are fifty-two and napping on the porch.
In Santa Fe, Fiesta night, an effigy burns gloom.

When the earth shifts into winter
and pageants of Jesus abound,
I walk out into the cold night to shut
the chickens. Coyotes are hungry now.

Nobody's job is perfect. My husband's
keeps him from sleep and from my thighs.
My daughter is in Nepal. My son living
in the limbo of age twenty-one. Only you,

my youngest, seem to ordain life, make
the ordinary holy. Studying mythology,
planning Halloween, watching boys enter puberty.
We're in old folk songs, "Pastures of Plenty,"
"America the Beautiful," hedging toward
Thanksgiving. Far from the killing fields of rice.

My brother hosts a strange affliction,
"I look like Phantom of the Opera," he says twice
on the phone, he who seldom repeats himself.
My friend from Chimayo has lost her brother,
cries in what was once Safeway. I love the shop
they own, *El Portrero,* with its saints and prayer cards.
My arms filled with groceries as a woman
in the parking lot tells me of her near-death

experience. I float back to my car,
flip death on its back and pin it there,
wrestling the angel of Española—
traction, accident, rodeo, cocaine,
heroin, fiestas, alcohol. This
parking lot filled—with all my relations.

There is white and there is whiter.
Silence you already knew. White noise
and empires of yellow leaves, chromium
in the cottonwood trees. If I were poised
like the crinoline of rock, corrugated
as sandstone, or trembling like aspen.
But no. I notice an old woman with a penny
in her loafers wearing loads of turquoise.

There is so much music in the White Place,
I think I hear Georgia O'Keeffe guffaw, I sat
behind her once in church. The rocks are tuff.
We never stop talking about beauty.
It is beauty that will do us in.
Today for a change I don't feel so old.

Seems I might live too socially, relentless
lunches, or too mechanically, car and computer,
and then die. Young people exit this valley
despite safe sex talks or films about suicide.
It's cars and guns, an occasional stabbing.
We living click our tongues in the old sound
for loss which means aren't we glad they aren't
ours. But they are, under veils of mileage and blood.

My daughter called from Nepal. I get to say
Kathmandu every day, it's where they flew.
She names the river they will raft down.
I am giddy on the phone, breaking up reception,
our voices overlap. Hers cuts up and clicks.
In the background men speak clear Nepali.

An old post card with a painting from India,
"The Night Pierces Me like a Sword."
I've still got the flu, even the blues
have to be put on hold until I get well.
I said my book will be called, No Plot.
I can be mean. Wish you were a pet
with adoring eyes, rather than professor
of a required course on say, statistics.

Of course I love, but it gets off track
reading D.H. Lawrence and Camus. My word,
your word, soon it will change from sword
to concubine to peace. I've seen the work
of change, the patterns of rice as it flies
from the hands of the guests at the wedding.

Thanksgiving Day and the word I feared,
"accident," came on the phone line from Nepal.
It wasn't my child but her friend, another
woman's girl riding on top of the bus.
After the trek wild-handed fate missed you,
smacked her clear to emergency. Dire
straits shock us from the other world
where nothing we do here matters. I baste

the bird we raised and killed. Arrange flowers
in the face of life when the wires are taut. Night
in Pokara is filled with my daughter's tears:
"It was like a Freddy Kruger movie. I'm no good
with blood, we kept her out of shock.
Is it Thanksgiving ?" she asks in fright.

She came back from Nepal with a pierced
nose and a certain heart. Last night I dreamed
her feet were painted henna and black
as if for marriage. Her head shaved
as if for ordination. She and her sister
ate rice, had one body spanning years.
I live on edge. The henna cost dearly, or so
I dreamed, and would be danced off in days.

I saw her alive and fine, felt ancient weariness.
Her zest and my fear, her face and my fate.
Moved not to tears but to the fire where I sat
by her, and sat, drank ginseng tea for strength
and filled the night with thanks. Prayer
leaked into the night from my amateur heart.

Is the world New? A thousand starlings found
my feeder. My youngest has the flu.
My husband crashed on the couch, we missed
the bonfire, the party, didn't even kiss.
My son and I discussed militias, over-
population and starvation. Our terrible American
refrigerator is full, everything from lox
to fried rice, leftover Chinese, Mandarin

or Cantonese I don't know. In childhood
the world was new though the sky stank
with industry. It's clean here, radiation
doesn't show, no idea what we inherit.
Read and watch the tube, walk and sleep too much.
Like a bear, we have caves, like a *sadhu*.

I cut my hair. You shave off your mustache
in sudden gesture. You give birth to a lip
upper and tender, the thin unkissed part
of yourself. Our daughter shrieks, never
saw you look so young out of the brush.
All day she reacts loudly. I find my love,
the old one I took to bed, took to wed,
drove from Chicago to the coast, silent.

At work people are split, those who hate
or like, those who don't notice. The women,
always the women, how they love in ways
I can't imagine. We love in ways the world
will never see. Now your lips are revealed,
the line from birth to death filled with kisses.

He dreamed he was happy holding me
with a different head. I dreamed a baby
with a smile. Is there blame here?
A baby skips across a river like a stone,
four skips. Smiling. All rivers lead
to the Rio Grande, which is not so grand,
only west. Identified flying lives,
the river lifts from its bed, a ribbon

to tie the gift wrapped as landscape.
Another layer of forgiveness, another round,
flat stone. Another belly laugh, a baby.
The laugh of the river. Clear happiness.
A coin. A stone skipping across heaven.
A river falling exhausted into bed.

What is the matter with you? All I want
is a new life. Spring winds blast hyacinth.
The president wants someone to get him off.
Separates his actions from his pants.
"Is there a new kind of person with no idea
what he or she has done?" my friend asks.
"You must change your life," Rilke replies
in translation from the German past.

"I have wasted my life," James Wright
insists from a hammock. St. John's Wort
for the blues. Can't get no satisfaction.
Like I say, if you can't get ahead, get
even. Him and me go way back. Back
to the first case of spring fever.

Sho' nuff, they say down south
by the Atlantic. I'm hardly alone.
My mother's breathing stains the air with snores.
Her glib daughter, I praise her noisy mouth,
browse through old photos, absorb her love. Phone
you. Toss all night, elbow to future grief.
Her heart's beat eighty-five years. My belief
systems are wide open. I'm in the zone.

Love past has been clumsy, antsy *amour*.
My father's store, tailors stitched love's long seams.
I was an only girl, a radical daydream.
They'd clothe me in pink, but I was leather.
He died informally, no tux or cummerbund.
Hollyhocks monogram summer. He is my dark sun.

The phone call came after we played
Scrabble. I won, which made you lose.
You had expressed an interest in *amour*.
For the third night I had served rice.
The phone rang when I was in bed
reading a book called *Folly*, thinking
how much life goes into a quick read.

"Bad News," a fiction writer said.
"We thought you'd want to know, Jim Sagel
is dead." I knew by whose hand before
he said. Words like *rosary* and *funeral*
have come of late into my bed. I answered
the phone of loving you as best I could.

I heard this morning that lobsters
were more prevalent than ever in eastern seas
and that can mean decline of a species.
Right now I want to fuck constantly.
Does that signal or signify demise
of our rather old-fashioned fuckeree?
I am so angry, darling, I could spit.
So irate, I might leave you to your own bisque

with Swiss horse women, beaver traps
and booze. Oh darling, it is midnight
and I can't snooze, have no idea of your
whereabouts. I find omens in the mail,
magic eight ball, metaphors, black widows
by the door. Just this week I posted bail.

Our daughters heated up rice. You rode
a horse through a gale. The wind was fierce
and flattened my fine mood. The words jail
or hospital, my friend advised, cross a line,
a track I don't want to live across. Bad side
of the news, shady side of the block.
Lock, stock, and barrel, time's in hock.
Night before the graduation of our son.

I do not quibble with fun, ride this anger
as you rode our old untrustworthy mare,
or gelding not quite trained. You bring me pain
and a steamed-up serving of fresh pain.
I bear you like a cross, so Catholic.
I hate remorse and your gain, my loss.

Nobody took notes on the last hours.
And I did not document the past,
so neither the joy nor the agony
is inscribed, the jealousy, the drunken times
or the devotion. The birds on the radio sing.
Our daughter coughs downstairs.
We cried two hours and loved the last.
My path is the small path. Your large heart.

We found a dozen angels between us, one
old Jew residing in Israel and a Swiss woman
who once worked in a bank. I am grateful.
I think of John and Yoko Ono. I think of them
and their lyrics about Egypt. All the thank yous.

Diego, Henry Miller, Paul Gauguin.
Dylan Thomas, you want the *bon vivant*
and I've been trashed. Yet how lucky we are
to be alive, the weather unseasonably cool,
while we make love all night, fight knock-down-
drag-out fights. I watch your face grow beautiful.
You say, it's Her that made it so, the Other,
Swiss undercover agent in scant garb.

It's everything, midlife, skirt chase, sex.
It's soul work, old song, joke, cliché,
like "Sweet Young Thing." I grab the I Ching,
pull Tarot, read runes, swirl leaves in tea.
Some would grab a gun. What men want
wives do not provide. It's not me.

It isn't a time of nice nice on this lamenting planet.
You say you want to live as Rumi and Kabir did
yet rise tomorrow, dress again for work.
You cannot do the good good forever. We all
need waking. Me, by angels from the other side,
and you, by those on horseback. You're off again
in rain and thunder next to a woman on a horse.
She jumps over the house in one fabulist stride.

I am so ordinary, small life, large ego,
make no apple pie, but made three new
egos into bodies, a cup of Chai, America
the bottomless, from sea to shining shoes.
I watch TV a lot, overeat all day
waiting, like a shrew, for you and You.

We've been to the Holy Land and back, only you
don't recall anything. I asked you to give up
alcohol, the promise of sex with another woman.
What I must give up is large also, my thoughts
of betrayal these last months. The scenarios
of your wings over my pricey heart. Sorrow.
Chocolate, too, I surrender and my angers.
What's to come nobody knows. You call

and you are questioning the calling. What men
want is the question nobody else can answer.
I tell myself the story "What Women Want."
Sir Gawain and the ugly dame, that's me,
he's you, beautiful by day or night. We choose
and choose sovereignty or everybody loses.

Glorious crisis. Is it over now? My lover,
called husband, called spouse, is over
with the other he has grown to love. Not that way,
but it could have been. I could have had it play
out before me like opera. I'm not sobbing arias.
I'm not watching the clock while he visits her.
He is not Sinatra, gotta have it his way, not
Henry Miller, not a character in a play.

Are we out of the woods? The conversation
has begun that will carry us into a version
of ourselves that is not old news. Gotta have
action for the story to travel, not enough plot
here, too much bed and lyric. Marry a poet
to a man of action, watch it weave or unravel.

My son called from Oregon. I had to be
a mother and tell him about phones and energy,
how you have to give it to the phone, smile
into it, leave messages with life so while
others can't see your handsome face, they hear
the dear you are. Love by phone. Or drear
communiqués. He laughs. I am learning from Her how
to give information without advice. Thanks, Other,

with your nothing, your appealing young nothing,
you've woken me out of the matron swoon. Drought.
I'm praying for Fourth of July rain. They did a round
dance at San Juan, we left after the green corn.
You finally heard the drum behind the lines of dancers.
I had been telling you, but you have to hear it yourself.

Rode badlands with a woman my man
loves. I fell for her too, her warrior seat.
Watched her legs grip the saddle, ride the horse
into its spookiness. "There is nothing
he needs, and nothing I can keep from him,"
Akhmatova said. I want him to have everything,
the word compromise, a miser more than promise.

I am the wife. The bounty is now, the moment
rises and falls in a face. I have been fasting
from love. I want the real feast. I accept
nothing less. He craves a life off the lawn
and into the woods. I eat him alive. Student,
householder, *sanyassin*. We all go back
to the Mother. I am no longer her.

Gersh gave me permission to write any kind
of sonnet I want, "Just write a fuckin' sonnet."
And Grolnick says, in a riff from death, "Go, chick,
go." And Robert says you'll never meditate, stop
kidding yourself. And Rick inquires after my health.
Just write a sonnet, forget abba abba cd cd cd.
They all assemble in these fourteen lines,
give me thumbs up. Go ahead, the dead said.

My living love lost his job, cut off all his hair,
drank love in a beer. Wanted to trade romance
in for a new model. Rode off, over there.
I flipped. I did the Change of Life dance, sang
"Growing Old in America" blues. I cried myself down
ten pounds. Weight returns, but the dead cheer me on.

Hamlet last night, sat on the ground, your
head in my lap. Country matters. We come
to the city. This morning we love through
the blood and the history. I adore you, chum.
You are my asymmetry, my skyline, my soliloquy.
Today we saddle up and ride into the present
under an alien sky, Chimayo has never been so private,
the cars dream by, the horses calm, and you and I

a past and future riding down the road
to the Santuario for healing. I buy stickers
of the Virgin, you talk with women you don't know.
Apricots drop from the trees by our children's old
school. The three R's, romance, rehash, relax.
I've waited my whole life to star in this play.

I fly off to visit my old home. Call you each
day. You're wrestling with jealousy, a new man
in Her life. "Possession," you decide. Want Her
to be happy. There is no romance, you say.

I have no idea what we possess apart,
or together, alive and half gone. You are mine
or not, nobody can predict. I offer a climate
filled with food and sex and art.

You aim for the mountains, read of Africa,
want more and more. Explain how the brain
evolved in so few million years, and it takes you
time to grow your wings, get a passport to a life
apart from family. I am amicable, a word for divorce.
Don't go there. Mediation. Lawyers. Holy life-force.

Tree of heaven, ailanthus, slum tree I used
to call it back in Pittsburgh, womb of my
womb. On this road named Placita, I must
look it up, where I walk two miles each
day since The Shit Hit the Fan, Oh, excuse
me, The Conversation Began. Anyhow, flax
is in bloom and yellow ones too, blue
for me and outrageous for you. I'm okay

my neighbor tells a friend, and actually
I am better than that. Moon messed around
with clouds last night, corny sunset. I found
no new words for horny in the thesaurus.
Am I living in the blessing or the curse?
Choose blessing, though am wont to expect the worst.

Left Pittsburgh yesterday, city of steel
no more, gateway to my west. Man
in a yarmulke works at the kosher deli,
named Jumbo since he's full of baloney.
Aren't we all? Read at Rodef Shalom, got to pray.
Saw cousins, rabbis, saw my mom, my bro,
Don Carlioni of the clothing Mob. Flew TWA.
Two flash floods here at home in as many days.

Life is impossible, that's what keeps it real.
Watched *Lonesome Dove*, held hands, made love.
Best Eden I'll ever feel. You the smartest Adam.
I'll get you a car radio, installed. I'll buy
salami, spices, halvah, tongue. East
meets best, young man, I'm still enthralled.

Yesterday, eve of my birthday, I changed
my tune. I turned the word "crisis" in,
said "our marriage woke up." Drove alone
to a country zendo set among pines, bears, raccoons.
I drove east. I drove west. Sang my way home.
I canned the last peaches of the first tree.
I loved. I tried very hard not to hate.
I cut the biggest cabbage for my friend.

I cried until I had to leave the walls
see the stars. My beloved woke up. We sprawled
on the hood of our car and marveled,
named what we could, allowed its comeliness
and wash. We looked up,up. The sensei said,
"This Open Eye Ceremony has no beginning and no end."

You talk with your hands. I ask with my eyes.
The answer is the question, is there love here?
This phase, this glitch of mere life without ceasing.
I sat on a bench with a widower, his love
died, yet you would make a distance of me.
Distant peaks and Amazon, underwater depths.
Coyote would have woken me at four
had I been asleep. My old familiar, loneliness.

You are at a movie with the season's sweet treat.
My daughter on the Internet alone. I was swatting
flies in the name of the unspeakable.
The one eye of the fan wags back and forth.
The summer heat came late. Our daughters watch.
You are their imprint. Their imprimatur.

Dead rattlesnake shaped like an ampersand.
Before my walk I chased the rooster in,
the white one marooned outside the fence.
Fed the horses from loosely stacked hay
you got for free. Today's sunrise you'd pay
money for, board a plane, walk the beach, buy
a postcard just to see and say, I saw. Today's
your day, scraps of pain fly in and out of me.

But we can speak of it, and I keep peace,
can my peaches. Old hippie chick. I love the way
summer has gone, our child is back in school
and you and I are wiser, more and more
two Sixties lovers, holy moments, stoned
conversations, wakened, whacked-out fools.

On the portal, knocking open marriage,
remodeling the inner, you spoke to me of chaos
theory. Your head wedded the cottonwood and sky.
Instead of man and thought, there was leaf and vision,
space and brain. I blinked and you vanished,
breaking sky where idea belonged. I tried
to concentrate on chaos, the words whirred
from your enthusiastic mouth as you melted,

grew beyond logic, into transparency.
"Magritte" you said when you were solid, back.
It wasn't art, a door opening into sky,
it was the sky opening a man, the space it made
in you was huge and later you occupied a space in me,
entered my emptiness, passing in between the blue leaves.

When we are ancient and arousal is distant
as Hungary or Egypt or Nepal, I can remind you
how great the loving was for us last night.
It will still be current, electric man on magnetic
woman, not to impress or please, we are beyond
that, but pleasure in the pulse, loving every way.
You gave me two hours out of the heart
of the night, woke from your dream of manta ray.

Maybe we'll be in Crete, longing for this summer
in La Puebla, the sacred destination is now.
I love that women love you, double-edged sword.

Yes Ulysses, yes Cartier Bresson, I document
these moments we took for ourselves, a season
out of time to align, so far from bored.

Things are not as they seem. A blue
toothbrush in the bathroom between
the husband's and wife's belongs
to a young woman who opened a door,
rode a gray horse, flew over a house, knocked
both hearts, hers and Hers, his and hers, Hers
and his. A new story tells itself on their land,
so much forgiveness and yet things broke.

Is it good, bad? I don't know.
A Japanese monk in an old tale says,
"Is that so?" when a young woman claims
it is his baby and after he has raised it,
pays him another visit, admits it is another's.
Hands her the child, again, "Is that so?"

Nothing happened, I fought the Bhagavad Gita,
threw I Ching. A marrying maiden stirred the pot,
entranced the neighborhood. I was irate.
I watched my husband on the porch talk
to Her as if I weren't there. I was not
there. Nothing happened, he was sweet
on Her, not unfaithful, he was not faithful.
Love and sadness served on marriage plates.

We ate and ate one summer en pleine aire.
We feasted on ourselves and it was good.
We ate ourselves alive and went for more.
We entered each other's body knife and fork.
We fucked until the ocean banged the shore.
We asked which wine accompanies this food.

After Day of the Dead I say, "intimacy."
The word "sex" is too direct from me to you.
I can ask with my body, nestled or pushed,
but not easily with my mouth, unless kissed.

The full November moon after a week of rain.
My intelligence returned for a time. Now it's winter.
Forgive, forget, let go. Some threesome
of words! She lives below us on our land.

Her Paso Fino horses up to their fetlocks
in mud. Our horses displaced to a pen.
You call me "a keeper" to show your love.
The first time is endearing, but by the third
I want to break again with summer's last pain,
harvest the anguish behind that word "keep."

Inside a marriage is a sealed thing,
the envelope of self we push and sonic boom
light years beyond our best intention we meet
the love we spoke of when we were young
and vowing to do better than others had
in the impossible matrimonial alchemical
vessel. Long moan of staying home, not straying.
What were you saying? Stability can be disquieting.

Our change filled with omens and perdition.
How many flickers fit on the head of a marriage?
The cats make quick work of one and by evening
you chase our grown son with the bird's head. Today
in my daughter's hand her green tree frog, miraculous
all these months, living on nothing, like a saint.

In the car we asked how to find ground
when all is groundless. This at seventy
miles an hour, heading east to Las Vegas. I say,
though the land is steadier, we make our home
in another human. Far less reliable. All the while,
as you and I talk about death and craziness,
Ella Fitzgerald is singing. Under everything
a woman's voice murmurs about love.

I am trying to find myself, back in from the woods.
The car that won't start without a man in my arms.
I'm no model for the feminists. I dispatch a memo
to Mexico, *I'm coming, southern clime.*
I gamble, heart casino. Impossibly retro
while Ella's scratchy, ruined voice is ground.

In my New Year's dream a woman in a tent
gives me sandalwood oil, tells me I am
a prostitute. "I know," I say. Instead
of death's tunnel I travel a corridor
of Mexican vendors selling paper flowers,
souvenirs (I do not want to die), mementos
of riotous colors. "Spends money like a whore
at a carnival," my father said about my mother.

I wake, sniff for sandalwood. Surprised that after
a surfeit of sex you touch me. What a year!
Alcohol, a woman with turquoise eyes, horses,
New Mexican sky, job loss, talks deep as erotic thrust.
Three hours on any given morning, employed in depth,
love makes us offers from her gypsy tent.

Our car returned from Her. Each conversation
driving while intoxicated. When the dust settles
what's left of us? I ask, what's driving you from me?
We drive to Santa Fe, city of Holy Faith. Your head
turns east, eyes out of the car. I keep my eyes
ahead to wage the holiest war. You heard. Your head
looks to the mountains, like Martin Luther King,
like Jesus, Moses, any man wants more

than the intimate. I understand. Stand
by my man, as you have stood and sat and lain
by my alien shore. What am I driving at?
I ask for more. Small consolations of snow
flaunt the Sangres. Sunset's energy stuns.
Elation is out there, abroad, at least not guns or blows.

A jot of rain after drought. I miss
winter which has not graced us with a trace
of snow since two moons. I mean the cows came
home today, herded by the men on feisty horses.
Hackamore, lather, saddles and chaps. We've come
home through the gate as well. No more hell,
hallelujah. How many days did I waste
hollering down wishes into your wishing well?

But the past is paste, and the next move
is round-up, wrangler of this life, rope
it in, tie 'em up. Be happy. I kiss
every single part. Nothing is spare, love.
The life we hope's now being cast,
Tarot, therapy, astrology, Swiss Miss.

Holy text of a land we settled on
by the River Santa Cruz, in the wake
of the Sangre de Cristos. We live
on the thin crust of the present.

A moment inside a moment,
breaking the daily heart. All four directions
converge in my kitchen. Bread and eggs. Glasses
of water. My youngest child brushing her hair.

Don't give me no need, greed and fear.
Can't get no satisfaction, sounds like
a personal problem. Men and women inhabit
each other like undergarments. He wears me
and I wear him. "Don't try this at home,"
he says of our wild year.

The love month, the extraordinary departs
and we're back to ourselves with normal
American hearts. So I brood, pick a fight,
get the blues, yell when riding a horse.
I get scared, retreat, spoon up Haagen-Das.
We graduate from our crisis therapist.
All weekend I monitor your heart for a kiss.
At the movie, *Shakespeare In Love,* hold hands.

Nothing nothing nothing, this life of sanity
is all we have, and plenty enough for me.
How about you, looking for a job, how
about you, tracking politics, how about
you, underneath the car or the marriage bed?
Have you found normalcy or your edge?

I was born to a family in retail, have spent
life wanting a good fabric, a nice seam.
Did I choose to make nothing of this life?
I drive south, past Miami, clutching
the small wheel at my chest, sure I will die.
Or will I go on living beside Española,
a large woman without savings or make-up?
I am nothing, if not grateful. Thank you, Beti,

Harry, Carl, brother who prayed for me
and named me. Thank you three children treading
time, my feet still kick up a little. Man wearing
a husband noose, thanks for strangling the lover.
Wheel of fate, fortune, wheel of karma. This traffic
is thick and fast. We are spun by the Other.

It would have been enough, *dayenu,* the singing
and the letting my people go. Moses has attitude.
Elijah on a Harley. Men make trouble and women
write and direct some other holy film. This life is shot
in living color. Spring greens, an egg, horseradish
pinked by beets. The beat goes on, and the beat
generation dies. A musical called *Hair,* one called
Jesus Christ Superstar. I'm just about done with these.

Last night Passover made out of the please
and the thanks. Missiles fly to Kosovo,
get shot down. Surprise, the faces of Albanians
are just like love! War and peace fly over my garden.
We are flung in and out of Eden. Who bit the apple?
Who knew what trouble was brewing?

Last weekend, two French films on video.
The Lovers where a young Jeanne Moreau
takes a lover when she already has a lover.
I didn't see the end, asleep under the covers.
You said nothing happened, they did it in the road.
Don't try this at home. Your skin primed to explode.
We made it, just barely, I was ripe to quit.
My oxymoron married to your hyperbole, my paradox.

Socks under the bed, monotheism, a couple on a roll.
Detach, let go, my books on codependency extol.
Your dichotomy is married to my monogamy.
Non-duality is courting pantheistic animal husbandry.
The Shema says, Listen! oh God wrestler.
So, what say, glad you got me and not Her?

A woman I only know well enough to love
is dying in a town I don't want to live in.
I speak to her husband as she sleeps.
Impossible fate, who invited death
here into his mother-in-law's house?
That he is a pharmacist by day, cures
dispensed, does not make this easier.

He was a boy in India who hadn't met this girl
were they preparing for this, early death,
a bowl of grief for dinner, *dahl, raita,*
fruits as sweet as tidbits served Ganesh?
Life offers her sweet face to certain death.
She is fed to the gods for *prasad.*

for Kalpna

Most beautiful half-moon I've ever seen.
Remember when we slept on the trampoline
to watch shooting stars? You knew too much.
Meteors, made of fire and gas, the sky is such
magnificence. It was crazy then and now
you're back to work, on line, in tow.
My heart broke and healed. I take estrogen,
a woman flirting with death, God knows my sins.

Dark by your breath, right now, at half past three
I inhale, widow cat reclines on me
clawing with love, the way they do, and purr.
After all, normal threatens to further.
The books from crisis still line my bed.
I read for pleasure, forget my old head.

Are you still carrying the woman across
the stream, the Zen master asked his student.
I am still carrying a woman across a summer,
across a year, over the soil in my garden.
The woman is smoking American Spirit
cigarettes, has no working papers, money,
can't afford our car which we would gladly
sell her. She's driven it all year.

When I was sick with fear a doctor said
men are only worth so many tears.
The woman has blue eyes that match my dear's.
My husband said, "Give me three months, then you
can have me back." My face in the mirror is cracked,
still carrying all these real and imagined facts.

My son drives off to Oregon in a black Toyota
truck loaded with all his stuff. I wave and jump
in front of the greenhouse, the I'm gonna
miss you dance. "I don't care what your mother said,
you're a terrific guy," I tell him, hoping
to counteract my words that made him doubt.
We took a walk, talked about how two score
years ago I was in labor on this very road,

he rode a bike, was nine, I clowned and breathed
Lamaze and like an ancient woman on TV
who said, breath is the secret, inhale, ex.
She seemed wise, funny, they all do, the fit
and long lived. That baby came. Now you leave,
I throw kisses, cry, pray that you'll never die.

Last week I took a vow not to complain.
Those who know me laugh. I say,
"Complaint is the national anthem of my mind."
Learned that by inflection I can sneak one in.
"I have a lot to do" can swing both ways.
Try again to get over my phenomenal good luck,
move on through its partner, bad. Plant
eggplant and tomatoes for yin. I plant thyme.

Onion sets for yang, though they don't mind
if I complain or no. Went to a zendo,
spoke ancient chants for Mother's Day. The fly
on the window just is. No problems here,
a perfect world. My patience, a fine scar.
I bring my hand to my lip. I refrain.

You gave me roses and hoses, Happy Lover's Day.
Hope born on Mother's Day, a fortnight of years,
in glasses, braces that perfect her. I found myself
this morning on the vertical shelf of tears.
I knew I'd won some battles, lost the war.
Alien Other voice out of the old terrain. We rode
our horses out. We rode them back, talked
about duality and non, past hoodoos, about lack.

Meanwhile, my daughter, center of my mind
carries birthday flowers from her friends.
Her life, a fortnight: world without end.
World without friends is worse. Hers gave her
a lunchbox with Kali, divine red tongue
lapping up time. For now, I pretend she's mine.

I served up lettuce thinnings in the rain.
Last year they were the antidotes to pain.
This year, instead of eating Paradise
I taste the fear inside the delicate, rice
and chicken, meals like a uniform. Let us
be kind, each to each, wear our faces
before we were born. Shallot is queen
of sauces, the leek the king of soup.

I planted early, hope to harvest late.
Last night I tried to lure you on a date.
Nothing worked out, TV was full of pain, our show
sabotaged what little time we have. Your job,
my job, your trip. The finale of the year
of getting a grip, not the year of letting go.

You're in Alaska and I don't know what side
of the bed to get up on. Right, left, or wrong.
All year we fought dichotomy,
Yin, yang, good or bad, I water plants.
I walk Placita Road. Six magpies feast
on rabbit. Thoughts of the year trash my mind
like signs of drink litter this scenic whole way.
The acequia cruises like the blues long-

ing for water instead of love, requited, un.
I think that being married is not so much fun
as it is the cloister, convent of Holy You and, crass,
Impossible Me. Vice Versa. Ebb and Flo.
Those pesky vows and charming older pair.
No one warned how much would come to pass.

We talk about word origins at dawn,
"assassin" and "Dharma" over toast.
Life in this convent isn't half bad.
God is here, the kids, the Four Noble Truths
hang over my bed, but I don't read them.
The garden with snow peas, the porch,
the dishes, Father, Son, and Holy Smoke
Jacob accidentally said, but Catholic is no joke,

nor being a Jew which means from Judea
and from a long ancestral Hebrew line.
You and I met across a battlefield.
We looked, we kissed, we married, and are fine.
I like this convent for the food and views.
Sex is good also, if one gets to choose.

My son donated his ponytail for wigs.
Our eldest daughter's wings are silk.
The youngest turns womanly, drives my car.
The Other Woman moves to Albuquerque, though
Santa Fe scans better. The man works hard.
The bard takes out a contract to kill time.
The fruit comes on in drought, hallelujah.

Apricot, apple, plum, rice, crow, and sky.
Life turns a circle and the circle spins.
The gyroscope, the atom bomb, the Cerro Grande Fire.
The frog, the bull snake and the rattle shake.
Owl feathers spell out, *all of this must end.*
The call, the caller, desire, no desire.

On our anniversary at Santuario
I'm in the chapel alone. The altar
is laden with red and green striations,
gold filigree, so beautiful you could die,
but Christ is dying for you, a crucifix of woe,
large wooden rosary dangling
to his knees. I think of making love,
how you descend into Catholic.

Your soul fills your face and I could
be looking at a cliff face or clouds,
I could be looking into Aramaic or
a stranger, an oasis or the elemental table.
Love is best at distance or so close
the world tumbles inside us for solace.

Joan Logghe has lived in rural northern New Mexico since April 11, 1973, raised three children with Michael Logghe, and together designed and built three houses. Joan is poetry editor for Mothering Magazine, on the faculty at Ghost Ranch Conference Center, and recently taught poetry to students in Bratislava, Vienna, and Zagreb. Recipient of a National Endowment for the Arts Fellowship in Poetry, a Barbara Deming/Money for Women grant, Witter Bynner Foundation for Poetry grants, and a Mabel Dodge Luhan Internship. Robert Bly, her teacher, says of this collection, "I love the sudden changes in these sonnets. Things change fast as in art or life."

Kali is an aspect of the great goddess Devi, the most complex and powerful of the goddesses. Kali is one of the fiercer aspects of Devi, but nonetheless as Shiva's consort, she represents female energy. Kali's aspect is destructive and all-pervading, as she represents the power or energy of time. Her four arms represent the four directions of space identified with the complete cycle of time. Kali is beyond time, beyond fear...her giving hand shows she is the giver of bliss. Because she represents a stage beyond all attachment, she appears fearful to us. So, she has a dual aspect— both destroyer of all that exists and the giver of eternal peace.

This image is from drawings by women of Mithila, India.